An Evangelical Theology *for* Counseling

An Evangelical
Theology *for*
Counseling

Reflections on Twenty-three Years in the Classroom

Wayne Hatcher

WinePressPublishing
Great Books, Defined.

WinePress Publishing (PO Box 428, Enumclaw, WA 98022) functions only as book publisher. As such, the ultimate design, content, editorial accuracy, and views expressed or implied in this work are those of the author.

ISBN 13: 978-1-4141-2263-2
ISBN 10: 1-4141-2263-2
Library of Congress Catalog Card Number: 2011961731

Contents

Preface

I WAS TEACHING EDU 685, a course called
"Religion, Spirituality, and Diversity in the
Helping Professions." One night at break, a
group of students and I were talking about the fact
that the best texts for the course were written and
edited by Mormons, and how the book came to
be used in a course in a Baptist college. A divinity
student looked at me and innocently said, "When
are you going to write your book for this class?" I'll
confess that I felt a bit flattered by the suggestion
and filed it away in the back of my brain.

What is a "theology" of counseling? There has
been a lot written in recent years about the integra-
tion of faith and psychology and counseling. There
is a desire to do away with "either/or" thinking on

the seeming contradictions between psychology and faith. Everyone has a theology, and everyone has a psychology—each of us believes certain ideas to be true, and those ideas constitute our theology (ideas about God) and our psychology (ideas about man). We interpret our experiences through the grid of those ideas. Some people interpret all experiences from a theological perspective, some from a psychological perspective, and some with a more integrated view consider both. Many feel that the two perspectives should be kept totally separate. I have met all these types and more at conferences and meetings of counselors. I hope this book will encourage more counselors to develop a more integrated perspective that considers the theological perspectives as well as the psychological.

Bear in mind that when we talk about "theological ideas," we have to speak relatively when we use descriptors such as "conservative" or "liberal," as they may mean different things to different people. The terms really have more to do with the rigidity with which a person holds to a belief system than the belief system itself. Many conservative Christians are "evangelicals" who believe traditional theological ideas such as the deity of Jesus, Jesus' sacrificial death for mankind, and the Bible as the Word of God, but while they hold these firm beliefs, they will listen to other viewpoints. "Fundamentalists," on the other hand, will also hold some firm beliefs, but they will judge everyone who disagrees with them as wrong. In this sense, fundamentalism is not as much a belief system as it is an attitude.

Fundamentalists tend to be hard to work with because of their rigidity. When I was in the pastorate, a friend sent me a complimentary subscription to a popular fundamentalist newspaper. In the edition, the editor wrote an article condemning a fellow evangelist for uniting with a Southern Baptist church. Why? Because the evangelist supported a giving plan that he did not. I took issue with the editor, wrote a letter expressing my opinion, and asked for my subscription to be stopped. In the editor's reply, he told me that while I had a right to an opinion, I was wrong. He said he would not stop the paper because it was a complimentary subscription. Further argument was futile, so I went to the post office and had the paper stopped.

You will find liberal, conservative, and fundamentalist attitudes in all belief systems—they are not exclusive to Christian groups. In all of the writing that has been done about spirituality in counseling, very little has been written by or for evangelicals, and much of what has been written is fairly critical of the counseling profession. There is a gap in knowledge between many counselors and many Christians; they simply don't understand each other and don't listen to each other. I hope that this book will begin to bridge that gap.

Please do not get the idea that this book is just for Christian counselors to read; it will benefit any counselor who reads it. All counselors work with people of faith, and we all must deal with those issues whether we are prepared or not. If we take the approach that we are not sure about spiritual issues and don't want to talk about them, we will lose many of our clients, because these issues are important to them (in a 2006 Gallup poll, 84 percent of people stated spiritual issues as being important to them). We will also lose clients if we are viewed as being too dogmatic. We need to get in touch with ourselves and what we believe first, and then let our new awareness make us more compassionate as we listen to our clients tell their story.

Finally, this book is intended to be a primer to take readers where they have never been before. It is my hope that as you read this book, you will begin to see things in a different light than you might have considered previously. I pray that God will do such a work in all of us.

Note: When religion is referred to in this manuscript, the context is Christianity, unless otherwise specified. This is not to imply that these suggestions might not be useful even to a totally secular-minded counselor or a practitioner of another faith.

Part One

General Issues in Counseling

Chapter 1

My Personal Journey

LL OF US, to a large degree, are shaped by our early experiences. By this I mean that when we have an experience, we interpret it by our own unique perspective and then do one of two things: (1) if the results are pleasant, try to replicate the experience; or (2) if the results are unpleasant, try to suppress it. If we try to suppress the experience, we run the risk of subconsciously reproducing it later. What bold young parent has not said, "I'll never treat my children that way," only to find years later that they are doing the same thing? I call this the "Oh, my God, I've become Mom (or Dad)" syndrome. We might as well laugh at ourselves a little, because we have all done this at some point. We have also learned a lot of our religious behavior this way, which makes it harder for us to break away from those first teachings.

I was raised in a small Baptist church that loved Jesus and the gospel but had little trust of education—especially higher education. They believed that it was all right to have enough education to hold a job, but any more could make a fool out of a person. Higher education could lead to trust in self more than God, or even cause us to dare to question God, so we were taught not to think too much about certain questions. Our image of God was that of an old, gray-headed man who watched over us in the clouds. He had a long hammer, and He was just looking for times when we were misbehaving—including thinking the wrong things—so He could "bop" us on the head with it. Our church also had a very narrow view of the Bible. The only acceptable version was the *King James*. No modern translation was trustworthy. I was 25 years old before I stopped feeling guilty for reading the *New American Standard*.

I attended a state teachers' college and planned on becoming a math teacher and coach. I was on a football scholarship—sports was a big part of my life. I found myself surrounded with teammates and classmates from big cities and big churches, and my worldview began to broaden. I graduated in December 1972, taught briefly, and enrolled in Southwestern Baptist Theological Seminary in the fall of 1973. I graduated in December 1977 with a Master of Divinity focused mostly in biblical and theological studies. I taught for another brief period and then became pastor of Fayette Baptist Church in Fayette, Mississippi.

I spent four years at Fayette Baptist and six years at Scooba Baptist Church in Scooba, Mississippi. At Scooba, I was also part-time Baptist Student Union director and part-time instructor at East Mississippi Community College. Mississippi State University was only an hour's drive away, so in 1983 I enrolled part-time as a student in what I intended to be a second Master's Degree in counseling. That plan soon took on another shape, and I graduated in August 1987 with a Doctor of Education in counselor education, majoring in community counseling with a supporting area of psychology. A year after graduation, I moved to Campbell University, where I taught in the counselor education program for 23 years. After a 10-year struggle with Parkinson's disease, I retired from full-time teaching in May 2011.

As I have reflected on my experience, I realize that one thing that makes me different from many of my colleagues is the schools I have attended. I have had the opportunity to attend two world-class schools—one faith-based (Southwestern Baptist Theological Seminary) and the other science- and research-based (Mississippi State University). As a result, I have never felt that I had to pit one against the other as enemies. I have always viewed the two perspectives as looking at the world through different lenses, with different perspectives and assumptions.

The perspective with which we look at the world makes all the difference in what we see. For most of us, our perspective becomes our interpretive grid, and we see what we expect to see. I have learned much from both of the perspectives gained through my education, which has enhanced my understanding of human beings.

Reflection: What was your earliest image of God? Where did it come from? Did it scare you or comfort you?

Chapter 2

The Big Change

WHEN I FIRST began my studies in counseling, many students and faculty believed that spiritual values, spirituality and religion should be left out of counseling altogether—and ignored if possible. There were also faculty and students who saw spirituality as being too big a part of the human experience to be left out. There was a good mixture of both types at Mississippi State University.

At the time, this change in attitude was catching and gathering momentum. In his excellent book *Spirituality and Religion in Counseling and Psychotherapy*, Dr. Eugene Kelly documents the rise of this interest in religion/spirituality and answers two fundamental questions: (1) How did the relationship between the two get so bad? (2) How did it improve? We will deal with question number one first.

According to Kelly, although psychology in the sixteenth century had been friendly toward religion, by the nineteenth century it had become dominated by reason and the desire to be seen as a "science." This desire led to different assumptions. The scientific mind assumed that external forces caused all human behavior, while the religious mind saw mankind as having more choice in the matter. The association of religion with pathology was very damaging, and the professionalization of both fields led to further alienation as religion became the domain of the clergy and psychology became the domain of psychologist. The result was that religion became just as unfriendly as psychology, and counselors were not trained in how to work with spiritual issues (Kelly, 1995).

So how did things change for the better? What new conditions developed to improve the relationship between psychology and religion? First, Kelly notes that there has consistently been a prevalence of spirituality in American culture—according to opinion polls, the vast majority of people claim to believe in God. The majority rate their spiritual life from "very important" to "important." Because of this, many psychologists began to see the importance of addressing the spiritual needs of their clients.

Second, a growing body of empirical evidence demonstrated a link between faith and better health. While people of faith still got sick and died, they did so at a slower rate. They also tended to have fewer and shorter hospital stays and a better quality of life all around.

A third factor was the legacy of early counseling pioneers. Men such as Carl Jung, Alfred Adler, Charles Davis, and others had taken a holistic view of clients and considered spiritual values as part of that view. A fourth and final factor was a major paradigm shift in thinking that occurred from a modern worldview to a post-modern one. This type of mindset—though it focused more on subjectivity than objectivity—gave greater room for a faith perspective.

In 1997, the Association for Spiritual, Ethical, and Religious Value Issues in Counseling held a summit on spirituality. One of the primary items that came out of the summit was a set of competencies in spirituality that professional counselors could work toward (Horton-Parker & Fawcett, 2009). Like most lists of competencies, they were structured in behavioral terms:

1. The professional counselor can explain the differences and similarities between religion and spirituality.
2. The professional counselor can describe religious and spiritual beliefs in a cultural context.
3. The professional counselor can engage in self-exploration of religious and spiritual beliefs in order to increase sensitivity, understanding and acceptance of diverse belief systems.
4. The professional counselor can describe his or her religious and/or spiritual belief system and explain various models of religious or spiritual development across a person's lifespan.
5. The professional counselor can demonstrate sensitivity and acceptance of a variety of religious and/or spiritual expressions in direct communication.
6. The professional counselor can identify limits of his or her understanding of a client and refer the client to another therapist.
7. The professional counselor can assess the relevance and significance of a client's religious/spiritual expression in the counseling process as befits the client.

8. The professional counselor can be sensitive to and accepting of religious/spiritual themes in the counseling process as befits the client.

9. The professional counselor can use the client's religious and/or spiritual beliefs in the pursuit of the client's therapeutic goals as befits the client's expressed preference. (Horton-Parker & Fawcett, 2010).

These competencies are not intended for any one group. They are for us as individuals to measure our personal growth in this area.

In the mid-1990s, I developed a course called "Spirituality, Religion, and Diversity in the Helping Professions." It began as a course where students looked at different religions, their beliefs, and how to work with these groups in an ethical manner. We also discussed selected topics in the field. Over time, the course developed into a study on diversity from a religious perspective.

I began the class by asking the students to write down any questions they had about the topics at hand, and I promised to talk about these issues before the semester was over. I wanted to model transparency, so I made no attempt to hide my conservative evangelical beliefs. I tried to model humility by telling the students that "a little humility is always in order, for none of us is 100 percent right." I tried to model fairness by telling the students "there is truth to be learned from all religions, but my personal belief is that Christianity holds together better as a whole system of truth." My goal was not to be overtly evangelistic, but to challenge students to think seriously about the spiritual dimension of life and to think outside the box in ways they might not have been accustomed to doing.

In 2008, the American Counseling Association, along with the Association for Counselor Education and Supervision, sponsored a syllabus clearinghouse. Submissions were invited, and I sent the syllabus to this course. The small number of syllabi submitted in this area indicated a problem to me: Here was an area of human experience most psychologists generally agree is important, and yet we don't talk about it much. Why not? I personally believe that even though we have made progress in this area, we still don't have enough faculties who are trained in this area and feel comfortable talking about it. I don't believe a person necessarily needs a degree in religion to understand theological concepts, but he or she does need a commitment to study and grow in self-understanding.

It is for this reason that I have written this book. I hope to bridge the gap in knowledge and to challenge readers to think new thoughts, to grow in their awareness of spiritual issues, and to use that new awareness as a springboard to new growth. Based on student evaluations and self-reports, I can say that almost every semester I held the course I had someone decide to take his or her spiritual life more seriously.

Two of my favorite quotes come from an old magazine advertisement for Reformed Seminary, at that time located in Jackson, Mississippi. The first is, "[God] came to take away our sins, not our minds." The second is, "If you want to know the mind of God, you must learn to use your own." We do not need to be afraid to think. God is honored when we use our brains for their intended purpose. (If you wish to read further on this subject, I have included the reading list from my course as an appendix. While not an exhaustive list, it is a good start.)

Reflection: Two different people can hold very different opinions for very different but good reasons. How do you react when you encounter someone who has a different opinion about a topic and seems to know more than you do?

Chapter 3

Counseling Theory

MANY PEOPLE DO not like the word "theory" because it reminds them too much of science and research. Theories are defined as sets of ideas that are not proven facts but have some explanatory power. The fact is that we are all theorists, for we all try to explain what we observe (at least to ourselves), and our explanations are our theories. Some of our theories are fairly useful—evidence can be collected and they can be tested—while some are not as useful, because none of those things can be done.

Choosing a theory is one of the most practical things a counselor can do. A theory gives a counselor some important ideas to work with, including:

1. A time frame on which to focus (past or present)
2. Content on which to focus (conscious, subconscious)
3. A means for evaluating progress (better decisions, more effective behavior)
4. Treatment suggestions

Sooner or later, a counselor is going to have to look at a client's problem from a theoretical perspective. Some will choose one theory and try to make it fit everything. However, because this is quite difficult to do (few theories are that exhaustive), most will take two or three theories that make sense to them and attempt to combine them into an eclectic mix.

Counselors have many theories to choose from. Among the oldest are the psychodynamic theories conceived by Sigmund Freud. These theories largely focus on a person's past and his or her subconscious mind. Freud, who was Jewish by birth, was never friendly toward religion—he considered God an "illusion." Other schools of thought include behavioral and humanistic psychologies (Jones & Butman, 1991). A number of other good theory texts are on the market, including one of the few written from an evangelical point of view called *Modern Psychotherapies,* by Wheaton professors Stanton Jones and Richard Butman.

Each discussion of a theory presents (1) a model of psychotherapy, (2) a model of personality as its foundation, (3) a model of health and (4) a model of abnormality. All of these aspects need to be discussed and compared to teachings from a biblical worldview. At this point, many people become confused and begin to look for "Christian theory" in order to do "Christian counseling." The term "Christian counselor" has actually been used quite a bit in the mental health industry to imply that Christian counselors are superior to other types of "secular" counselors. However, it is certainly worth the time to ask what we actually mean by this term.

I have done quite a bit of reflection about my training and beliefs during the last 23 years, and when I have been asked to explain the term and how to use it, I usually say something like this: Christian counseling as a distinct system does not exist. There is no theory or method that is *distinctly* Christian. Instead of "Christian counseling," we have "Christians who counsel." The counselor's values, ethics, and how he or she deals with a client are what make counseling "Christian," not whether that counselor can quote from the Bible or pray during a session. In fact, those things can be harmful if not done with thought and planning.

Christians who desire to do biblically based counseling must compare theoretical concepts with biblical teachings. Again, this is quite different from simply quoting the Bible to a client, which may or may not be effective—it involves finding counseling concepts that are directly endorsed by the Bible. For example, cognitive-behavioral therapy is very popular among Christians who counsel because of the biblical emphasis on rational thought and behavior, as seen in the following passages of Scripture:

> Be transformed by the renewing of your mind.
> —Rom. 12:2

> Put off your old self . . . [and] put on the new self.
> —Eph. 4:22,24

Many concepts of secular theories, while not expressly endorsed by Scripture, are also not expressly condemned, and the practice of these theories can be beneficial. An example is Carl Rogers's concept of unconditional positive regard, which is similar to the biblical concept of grace, God's preferred way of dealing with humans (see Rom. 5:7-8). Other theoretical concepts are neither supported nor unsupported by Scripture, such as Freud's three-part structural model.

Of course, there are some theoretical concepts that Scripture solidly condemns. In one instance, I encountered a client in a marriage counseling situation who, when asked what he wanted in his marriage, replied that he desired to preserve both his marriage and the adulterous affair in which he was involved. It would be very difficult for a Christian who counsels to work with a client who had such a goal.

Reflection: Some people think that counseling theory is mostly a function of counselor personality. What do you think? If theory is not a function of counselor personality, then what is it?

Chapter 4

The Counseling Relationship

DIFFERENT THEORETICAL APPROACH-
ES will place different value on the positive
or negative nature of the counseling
relationship. Obviously, there are different relationships in counseling situations—some better than
others—and it is inevitable that the counseling
relationship will become intense and personal.
Psychologists such as Carl Rogers believed the
counselor-counselee relationship to be a necessary
and sufficient condition of therapy. Others who
ascribe to behavioral theories do not believe the
relationship to be nearly as important. They feel that
the client's cooperation with treatment is the most
important factor, though they admit that clients are

much more likely to cooperate if they feel positive about the therapist.

Oscar Thompson, professor of evangelism at Southwestern Seminary, captured this emphasis on relationships in his book *Concentric Circles of Concern*. Thompson's first chapter was titled "The Most Important Word," and he made a good case that this word is "relationship." Thompson believed that the gospel advanced along *relational* lines following the model of concentric circles. People first shared their faith with those in their closest relationships (represented by the innermost circles), and then with those in less-close relationships (represented by the outer circles). Although Thompson's book is not a counseling book per se, it illustrates the importance that some Christians place on relationships (Thompson, 1981).

People usually experience problems and/or pain in the context of relationships. Think about your own life and its ups and downs. How were your relationships during the "up" times? How were they in the "down" times? Because of this strong connection, I advise that my students get a good background in systems theory. Even though they may think they are doing individual therapy, there are always systemic elements (other people) involved.

Counseling is more than simply being nice to people, but I believe that the quality of the relationship between the counselor and counselee is very important because of the emphasis Christianity places on relationships. Of course, it will not always be possible for a counselor to build a positive relationship with every client. However, whenever possible, the counselor should seek to build a positive relationship with the client, for this relationship will give credibility to the counselor, and it can make the difference between success or failure. It is more than a pithy little cliché to say that our clients "don't care what we think until they think that we care."

Reflection: What does it say about our society that a person will pay good money to a total stranger for an hour of undivided attention?

Chapter 5

Empathy

IN CONVERSATIONS, WE often throw words around and assume that everyone knows what those words mean. "Empathy" is such a word. But what *is* empathy? It is not "sympathy," which is simply feeling sorry for someone. While sympathy may be the beginning of empathy in some people, it is really a lower level skill. A person can get bogged down in sympathy, whereas empathy can lead to productive action.

Empathy is a relationship-building people skill that is very important to have in counseling. It enables a counselor to understand a person's perspective on a given experience. Empathy can occur at the cognitive level—an understanding of what a person thinks about his or her experience—or it can occur at the emotional level—an understanding of how a person feels.

Which is more helpful? It "just depends" on the situation and the need of the moment. It has been my observation in teaching basic counseling skills that all people seem to have some capacity for empathy, but some have a much larger and more natural capacity for it. These students, who possess "people skills," make better counselors. This parallels the biblical concept of spiritual gifts, which states that God gifts certain individuals with the temperament, personality, and inclination to be a more natural counselor. This person may or may not have academic training as a counselor but can make up for that deficiency with natural gifts. The ideal, of course, is to identify these individuals and train them as counselors.

How does a person improve his or her empathic skills? By doing the work of *listening*. Many faith-based counselors—especially ministers with a story to tell—spend too much time telling clients what to do rather than just listening to their story. Jack Follies, my CPE/field supervisor, used to say that the hardest thing he had to teach preachers to do was "shut up and listen." It really does not matter what we have to say: *all counseling begins with listening.*

In the apostle Paul's day, the people often used instruments in pagan worship that made a very irritating sound. In the same way, until we have done the work of listening, we are like these "resounding gong[s] or clanging cymbal[s]" (1 Cor. 13:1-2). As counselors, we must listen *first*.

Reflection: Some people (myself included) believe that empathy is more a gift than a skill. What is the difference? How can you get more of the gift?

Chapter 6

Ethics

ONE OF THE most frequent ethical offenses committed by both spiritual and non-spiritual counselors is imposing, rather than exposing, their religious/spiritual beliefs and values. This is particularly true of counselors who have an evangelical faith. We have an urgent message to give (the gospel), and sometimes we let the gospel complicate the lesser issues. For instance, it makes little sense to say to a person, "I don't know what your problem is, but I know the answer—it's Jesus!" There is a time and place for witness, but therapy is not always the best context for it.

Several years ago, a local minister referred a client to me whom I'll call "Mary." This lady was suffering from depression, and a big part of her problem was her marriage. Mary had been widowed at age 35 and had a much idealized view of her first husband. Her second husband was domineering and verbally and emotionally abusive. They were both in their 60s and had been married for a number of years, and both were strongly committed to the Baptist faith.

Mary had gone to a therapist in a nearby city, who told her she would not get better until she left her second husband. Mary was offended that a therapist would make such a suggestion and immediately stopped seeing this counselor. The therapist's mistake was in imposing her values on Mary, who was a woman of strong religious conviction about marriage. She gave Mary no choice in the matter!

I worked with Mary for about six months, always with the assumption that the marriage bond was sacred and would not be broken. Mary and I worked on issues *within* the context of the marriage bond. In subsequent chapters, I will outline some of the steps we took and how the counseling relationship progressed.

Reflection: How could Mary's first psychiatrist have handled this situation differently?

Chapter 7

Faith and
Self-Esteem

THERE IS A significant controversy going on in the field of psychology over the issue of self-esteem. Basically, the traditional self-esteem advocates feel that self-esteem is everything to a person: health, happiness, the basis of mental health, and so forth. The non-traditionalists, while not opposed to a person having high self-esteem, insist that it can be inflated, unrealistic, and do more harm than good. Religious people are also divided, but for a different reason. Some believe that encouraging people to have better self-esteem means encouraging them to be selfish and self-indulgent. However, that is not how a psychologist would describe a person with high self-esteem.

Self-image is simply how we see ourselves, and self-esteem is how we feel about what we see. In other words, self-esteem is self-image with a value judgment placed on it. One psychologist, Mark McMinn, presented an ideal model of mental health drawn from the life of Jesus. McMinn pointed to an incident recorded in Matthew 22:34-40, where Jesus is approached by a man who asks Him, "Teacher, which is the greatest commandment in the Law?" (v. 36). This was actually an ongoing religious argument; the religious leadership of the day had divided the Law into positive and negative statements (things to do and not to do) and argued all the time over which was most important. Jesus responded by talking about relationships at three levels: (1) mankind-God, (2) mankind-self, and (3) mankind-mankind (McMinn, 1996).

One time, before I ever took my first graduate-level psychology course, I was studying this passage for a Sunday sermon at Fayette Baptist Church. As I looked at Jesus' response, I had a revelation that has since directed my ministry and my life. Everything important in life is *relational in nature*. No matter how pure our theology is, it is suspect if it does not lead us to love God, our neighbor, and our self. To me, what Jesus is saying is, "Take care of the important things; the rest will fall into place."

So, what does that brief interlude into biblical exegesis have to do with models of mental health and/or self-esteem? McMinn proposes that a balanced personality will always have three things: (1) a balanced sense of need for God and others, (2) an accurate sense of self, and (3) healing relationships. In regard to the sense of self, there will always be balance. We won't always feel on top of the world, and we won't always be on top, but there will be balance and we will see ourselves as we truly are.

Reflection: Someone once said, "In life, take care of the little things and the big things will take care of themselves." What is a practical illustration of this from your own experience?

Part Two

Implicit Spiritual Issues in Counseling

Every day, counselors in all sorts of settings deal with vexing and perplexing *spiritual issues* that always seem to keep coming back to haunt them. Everyone has an opinion on them, but no one is sure of the answers. This section, though brief, discusses some of these implicit spiritual issues that are always present, though usually unspoken.

Chapter 8

Questions Counselors Ponder

IF A PERSON goes to a church-related counselor, he or she expects to talk about spiritual issues, and both the counselor and client should be prepared to do so. Counselors in "secular" settings, however, are often taken by surprise at a client's willingness to talk about spiritual issues. These counselors take several approaches to resolve the issue:

1. They refer the client to a "religious professional."
2. They assume such beliefs to be the problem and attempt to change their client's beliefs.
3. They deal only with psychological issues and ignore the spiritual ones.

4. They try reframing the spiritual issues into
   psychological terms.

The first three responses are inadequate, while
the fourth is difficult for the counselor to do if he or
she is not knowledgeable about the Bible.

Even though these issues may have surprised the
counselor—he or she was not expecting to have to
deal with them—they are basic questions to human
experience, and each of us should spend some time
thinking them through. Here are some of these basic
questions with which counselors often struggle:

1. *How much should a counselor self-disclose,
   especially about religious belief?* A counselor
   may choose self-disclosure. That is not inap-
   propriate, but such sharing needs to be kept
   to a minimum. In therapy, the client is the
   center of attention.

2. *How should a counselor deal with religious
   authority?* Religious authorities are significant in the lives of many people. What do
   counselors do when the authority contradicts
   them? Should religious authority ever be
   challenged? If so, which ones, and how?
   There's a multitude of sticky questions here.

3. *Can a spiritual counselor use psychological
   theory in counseling? Can a secular counselor*

use spiritual approaches? Can a faith perspective be integrated with a scientific one, or are they mutually exclusive?

4. *What is the worth of a person? How does that influence whether or not counselors work with clients to whom they are not naturally drawn?*

5. *What is the role of sin in human suffering?* The Bible teaches that sin is behind all human suffering in some way. It also teaches that people should not judge one another, because no one is perfect—and no one is smart enough to know specifically for what sins people are suffering.

6. *Can people change? If they can't, why bother?* Counselors need to hold some hope for people to change.

7. *What difference does Christ make?* Christians are a forgiven people, but they are not perfect. Counselors need to remember that we all are a people in process!

Readers will notice that for some (2,3,4)of these questions I do not offer concrete answers. That is because there are none. Answers depend on situations and the options available to both counselor and client.

Reflection: Which of these questions gives you the most trouble?

Part Three

Explicit Techniques and Interventions

This section contains a discussion of planned interventions and topics. Many of these can be used to address the unplanned topics that often come up in the course of therapy.

Chapter 9

Assessment

A COUNSELOR BEGINS an assessment the moment a client walks in the door. It is an ongoing part of the process. However, an immediate problem develops: assessment requires measurement, but how is something like spirituality measured? Some counselors simply measure spiritual/religious behavior, but it's really not that simple. Religious behavior can be overwhelmed by other circumstances, such as illnesses. It may also be part of a disorder, and the behavior may be detrimental.

Spirituality and religion are part of a larger context of a person's life. Generally, the more religious a person is, the more he or she will tend to have presenting problems intertwined with religious issues. This person will also tend to spiritualize most of his or her problems.

A few validated psychological instruments have been developed for this purpose. In his book *Spirituality and Religion in Counseling and Psychotherapy,* Dr. Eugene Kelly provides three assessment tools that are field-tested and validated: (1) the Spiritual Assessment Inventory, (2) the Index of Core Spiritual Experiences, and (3) the Spiritual Well-Being Scale. Some interesting work has also been done with the Myers-Briggs Type Indicator® (MBTI®) on personality type and spirituality. Of course, use of these assessment tools needs to be limited to persons trained in administration and interpretation of these instruments.

The most common spiritual assessment tool that most of us as counselors will use is a structured interview that includes questions about spirituality. Questions to ask in such an interview include the following:

1. Can you explain how your spirituality is *important* to you on a daily basis?
2. How do you *express* your spirituality every day?
3. *Why* are you spiritual? Is it possible to be spiritual for the wrong reason?

4. *What* are your basic beliefs, especially about God? How do your beliefs impact your daily life?

The emphasis is on the practical. We don't want our assessment to be an "I believe" list, but an indication of how spirituality affects daily life.

Reflection: How can you harmonize doing assessments of people with Jesus' command not to judge others?

Chapter 10

Dealing with Emotions

MANY PEOPLE (ESPECIALLY evangelical Christians) have a difficult time dealing with certain emotions—anger, depression, failure, love and acceptance, to name just a few. Experiencing a full range of emotional responses is a natural part of being human. Nevertheless, somewhere along the way we have gotten the idea that "good Christians shouldn't feel that way." As more "taboo" emotions are added to our experience, the message often becomes, "good Christians don't *feel*." Then we add in all the statements in the Bible about being "victorious Christians," and we set up a scenario in which we feel bad about feeling bad—and everything is compounded.

Earlier, I told you about Mary, a client referred to me by a local minister. Mary was not only depressed but also felt guilty about feeling this way, because in her mind Christians were not supposed to become depressed. She even dropped out of her Bible study at church because she was embarrassed.

I had been thinking a lot about the old Freudian definition of depression as "anger turned on oneself," and so in one of our sessions I had the following exchange with her.

Wayne: You must really feel angry sometimes with all the bad stuff you have had happen in your life.

Mary: I never get angry.

Wayne: What do you call it?

Mary: I just get frustrated.

Wayne: What's the difference?

Mary did not know what to say. We talked about the difference and Paul's guidelines for dealing with anger in Ephesians 4:26-27: "'In your anger do not sin': Do not let the sun go down while you are still angry, and do not give the devil a foothold." The idea that a Christian could be angry and not sin was a real revelation for Mary. She needed to see that Jesus experienced the full range of human emotion. She needed to see that emotions are morally neutral; it is what we do with those emotions that determines whether we sin or not.

Reflection: Think about a time when your emotions took control of you. What happened?

Chapter 11

Prayer in Therapy

IS IT APPROPRIATE for counselors to pray for their clients at the end of a session? It seems an appropriate thing for the Christian practitioner to do, but the question needs to be asked, "Is it always good to pray with a client? Is there ever a wrong time?" Surprisingly, Christian practitioners disagree on the specifics of how this should be handled. Some counselors pray out loud at the beginning of the session; some pray at the end of a session. Some therapists will only pray silently for a client, or pray for him or her outside the session. Some pray silently during the sessions.

Is it ever wrong for us as counselors to pray for a client? While I do not believe it is wrong to pray, I do believe that sometimes our timing in prayer can be wrong. My major concern centers around developing dependency on the part of the client and prayer becoming a substitute for legitimate work that needs to be done. I believe it is helpful for clients to know that the counselor is praying for them both inside and outside the counseling sessions, but they also have work to do that involves more than passive prayer.

There has been a great deal of research and writing in recent years by both orthodox Christians and less-orthodox practitioners about the efficacy of prayer. However, to date, no study of which I am aware has been done that compares the efficacy of prayer across different religious groups (for example, Christians vs. Muslims). No group can claim a connection to God more than any other, based on research. As a Christian, I believe that prayer makes a difference. However, I must confess that while at times I have prayed and God has done exactly what I have asked, at other times I have been left just wondering. I don't always understand the difference. There is an element of mystery with which we are sometimes uncomfortable.

Reflection: Do you pray for clients? If so, how do you do it? Should you do it?

Chapter 12

Spiritual Surrender

D O YOU LIKE being in control? Do you like the feeling of knowing what to expect? Most of us have at least some need for control. Some of us are downright control freaks! We simply cannot stand to not be in control. The biggest problem with this is that *absolute control* does not exist. Truthfully, we have limited control over other people and the circumstances we experience.

Real and total control is an illusion. It does not exist! Ask any parents, and they will tell you that they only have control over their children when they are in their presence. When they are not around, they have no control over how their kids will choose to respond when presented with a given situation. So it is with us; the only real control we have is over how we choose to respond.

A sense of being out of control is a major source of stress in our lives. In fact, it could be said that our attempts at coping are our attempts at restoring a sense of control. Psychologist Kenneth Pargament has studied the religious coping styles of different groups, and has identified four types:

1. Self-directing: Believes that God provides the resources people need to handle a situation and expects them to take control and responsibility.
2. Collaborative: Sees God as partner in the coping process.
3. Deferring: Believes that God is responsible for the entire outcome of the situation, not themselves.
4. Pleading: Actively asks God to solve the crisis (Pargament, 1997).

Of the four groups that Pargament identified, the one that was the most successful in coping was the collaborative type. It reminds me of a story I once heard about two boys walking to school. When they realized they were going to be late, one boy turned to the other and said, "Let's pray about it," to which his companion replied, "Let's run while we pray!"

Sometimes, it is necessary "to run while we pray." It is an open question as to whether or not God will do for us what we can do for ourselves.

Surrender is a powerful spiritual technique for change in our clients' lives. This process occurs when they begin to have an awareness of a greater good or value than the immediate situation. But how do they do this? A good way to illustrate it is through a "two circles" exercise. Give your client a sheet of paper with two circles on it, one labeled "things I can control" and the other labeled "things I cannot control." Have the client fill in the circles and then compare the two. The "control" circle will be almost empty, while the "no control" circle will be running over. It can be a stunning revelation for clients to see this on paper.

To get the client to understand the "greater good" in the situation, ask the question, "What is God's will in this?" Each of us must surrender to that awareness. Surrendering is often difficult for us because it implies some sort of defeat, but in a paradoxical way, we are surrendering to freedom and power. Getting the client to reach this point of awareness is really the most crucial part of the process. Surrender is almost a natural response to that awareness, and it will never take place apart from that awareness. As counselors, we can spend a lot of time exploring uncontrollable aspects of a

client's situation and how to cope with them. We
need to talk with our clients directly about how to
surrender, using their own religious tradition.

Reflection: How often do you find yourself out
of control? In what sort of situations does this
happen?

Chapter 13

Forgiveness in Therapy

HOW CAN WE repair a broken relationship? How can we change past experiences? Forgiveness is both a basic life skill and a universal need. Sooner or later, we all have a need to forgive or to be forgiven.

Many counselors object to using forgiveness in therapy because they misunderstand its true nature. Before we can really be objective, we must understand exactly what is meant by the word. First of all, forgiveness is *not*:

- Excusing a person's bad behavior
- Passive acceptance (e.g., peace at any cost)
- Self-blame (e.g., "It was really my fault")

- Necessarily associated with remorse or repentance on the client's part
- Necessarily associated with reconciliation
- Based on justice—Christians are told to forgive because *they* have been forgiven. When we need it the most, we deserve it the least.

What, then, is forgiveness? Forgiveness is the conscious choice a person makes to not hold a grudge or seek retribution for a wrongdoing committed against him or her. Forgiveness is based on *mercy* and is a commitment to not seek revenge. It is a commitment that must be renewed daily.

From a secular viewpoint, forgiveness is (1) part of Christian duty, and (2) therapeutically beneficial to a person, even if he or she believes that it is insulting to forgive the person who committed an act against him or her. From a Christian perspective, forgiveness begins with an understanding of the pervasiveness of human sin. All humans are essentially self-seeking, are equally fallible, are in need of forgiveness, and are equally undeserving of it. Viewed from this perspective, forgiveness becomes an empathic response to a shared human need (see Eph. 4:32; Gal. 6:2).

As a counselor, I had clients who were victims of abuse who reacted violently at the suggestion of forgiving the one who had perpetrated the acts against them. Some were insulted at the suggestion and flatly refused to so. My usual response to this reaction was, "Are you prepared to carry this burden strapped to your back for the rest of your life?" In such situations, I would talk with the client about how much energy it required him or her to maintain a grudge.

I experienced this firsthand in a former pastorate. I had made a special request of the deacons, and one in particular had taken such issue with my request that he inappropriately criticized me in front of rest of the deacons. I felt his response was out of proportion to the request and that we needed to talk about it.

I was quite nervous about going to his house the next day, but we had a good talk. We did not agree on the matter, but we heard each other out and, most importantly, we left respecting each other. As I drove away that day, I had spent so much energy in attempting to reconcile that I was totally exhausted. This is why I made the point earlier that forgiveness does not always result in reconciliation. For some people, reconciliation can only be on their terms; there is no compromise. You may not want to agree to that, but you can still extend forgiveness to that person.

Reflection: Have you forgiven everyone in your life that you need to forgive? If not, what is keeping you from doing so?

Chapter 14

The Bible in Therapy

MOST RELIGIONS HAVE a holy book that serves as the basis for its proponents' faith and practice. Muslims have the Koran, Mormons have the *Book of Mormon*, and Hindus have the Vedas and Upanishads. The Bible is the holy book of Christians, and because most Christians are familiar with it, the bulk of my comments will be concerning it.

I met a young man once who was interested in becoming a school counselor. He was about to graduate from a nearby seminary with a degree in "biblical counseling." I asked him about the nature of his program of study, and he said that they had been taught to ignore psychology and other social sciences and only use the Bible in counseling—all the answers that anyone ever needed could be found there. This is identical to the position taken by Jay Adams, a Presbyterian minister who taught that psychological training was not necessary. All a person needed to counsel was a Master's of Divinity and a Bible!

While I certainly do not want to put down biblical wisdom, I must point out that the Bible makes no claim to be anything other than a book of religion. To this end, here are five principles to be remembered in biblical interpretation:

1. The Bible should be studied both devotionally as well as analytically. God wants to speak to both our hearts and our minds. He can and will do so if we listen.
2. The Bible is primarily a book of religion, although in a limited way it does speak about other aspects of reality. For example, even though the Bible is not a psychology text, we can learn psychology from certain sections (such as the wisdom literature).
3. The Bible is a historical book. It was not written in a cultural or historical vacuum, and this context must be understood to properly understand the Bible.
4. Our humility should make us aware that our interpretations may not always be correct.

For example, to say to a person, "You don't believe the Bible" and, "You don't believe in a literal seven-day creation" are two very different statements.

5. Different interpretations exist because the Bible is of divine-human origins. God is the ultimate author, but He used human authors and oversaw its writing and inspired its content.

Because the nature of the Bible is human-divine, it requires careful interpretation. By "human-divine," I do not mean that its human authorship should be denied, but rather that God inspired and somehow supervised its content. For this reason, it is called "God's Word." The Bible contains both natural and special revelation. *Natural revelation* is what can be learned through study of books, nature, and so forth. *Special revelation* is knowledge that only God can reveal to people.

The Bible is best used as a book of encouragement to call people to be all they can be in Christ. However, some Christians use the Bible as a club to "beat" people into shape. Here's an illustration of what I mean. A church member once came to my door holding his daughter in one hand and a Bible in the other. He wanted me to show him some verses that said how much God hated liars and how He would burn them in hell. He had caught his daughter in a lie, and he wanted to give her the same treatment he had received as a child.

I respected his role as a parent and agreed that his daughter needed to be confronted about her lie, but I felt his use of the Bible left something to be desired. The father was not using the Bible as an instrument of encouragement to the girl. Rather, he was making God an object of fear.

As a counselor, it is important to have a healthy respect for the Scriptures, as they reveal knowledge about God that is not revealed anywhere else. You should study the Bible both devotionally and analytically, and follow a few guidelines when using it in counseling. First, go slow until you learn your client's level of biblical literacy. Paraphrase or explain passages of Scripture that you use with the client—don't just quote them. In addition, use the vernacular of the client, and avoid arguments about interpretations.

Reflection: When you read the Bible, what response does it most often draw from you—awe, conviction, gratitude, fear, or something else?

Chapter 15

Faith and Health

ANY, IF NOT most, of the clients you will see will have concerns about their physical health. There is a whole class of disorders, known as somatoform or psychosomatic, that express themselves primarily through physical symptoms but have no known organic cause. In fact, a growing field of specialization is in health counseling.

What does it mean to be healthy? Professionals talk about three dimensions:

1. Absence of pain vs. presence: In the absence of pain, what is present in a person's life?

2. Functional ability vs. degree of handicap: To what degree is a person able to do what he or she wants?

3. Subjective sense of peace in life: Obviously, being healthy is more than just not being ill.

For several years, there has been a growing body of empirical evidence linking people of faith with better health. As previously mentioned, people of faith tend to have fewer illnesses, shorter hospital stays, and a better quality of life all around. When we look at mental health, we find that people of faith are no worse off than those of no faith—and in some cases, healthier. Faith can also be a strong source of support in times of illness or at other times when life seems out of control, *if* people choose to let it be. However, faith can also precipitate a crisis if things do not work the way a person expects. It is God's prerogative to heal or not.

Given this, what do we say to those whose faith is wavering in a crisis state? What do we say when their faith is not working for them anymore? This is a place where a well thought out self-disclosure might be effective. In my case, 10 years ago I was diagnosed with Parkinson's disease. Like anyone else, I have had my good, bad, and better days with the disease. I have not spent much time asking *why*

I have Parkinson's or feeling sorry for myself, as I know that would accomplish little. My faith has been a huge source of support as I have consciously chosen to live with the disease.

How does my faith help? First, it helps me to face reality. I have a chronic, progressive disease that will probably get worse over time. However, each of us also has a terminal disease—we are human, after all, and if we live long enough, we will contract a disease. We will get something and die from it.

Second, my faith helps me to accept my limited control. As we discussed in a previous chapter, everyone likes to feel in control, but the truth is that we are in control of very little. Control is mostly an illusion; the only thing we can really control is how we choose to respond to life as it happens to us.

Third, my faith compels me to live in the present. I am reminded daily of things I can no longer do well because of Parkinson's disease, so I choose to focus on those things I can do, and learn from them. And finally, my faith reminds me that God still uses me . . . He has used Parkinson's as a refining tool in my life. I don't know where He will lead, but I know I must follow, for He alone knows the way. That is my story; it is different from yours. We all have a story to tell, for we have all experienced some kind of hardship, but lived to tell the tale.

So when is self-disclosure for a counselor appropriate and effective? There are several factors to consider. First, it is important not to share out of your own need, but to identify with the needs of the client and attempt to meet those needs. Second, any story you share should be long enough to make a point, but short enough to not dominate the conversation. And finally, whatever you share must be *your* story, not borrowed from another person. Don't kid yourself that the client won't know the difference!

Reflection: What is your story?

Chapter 16

Diversity and Lessons
I Have Learned

A S A TEACHER for the last 23 years, I found that I could not just compel students to learn. I had to model it for them as well. A good teacher is always learning along with his or her students. For this reason, I would like to conclude this book with some lessons that I have learned over the years. These lessons are applicable to counseling people of different faiths, but, like everything else I have tried to teach, they are applicable to life in general, and you will be enriched if you try to practice them.

The first lesson is that *people are different, and that is okay.* We live in a culturally and religiously diverse world. It did not used to be that way—America was once known as the "great melting pot," where the identities of diverse groups melded into one. Today, however, America is more comparable to a tossed salad; all the ingredients are there, but they maintain their separate identities.

"Diversity" is a big word right now in academia. We are supposed to celebrate diversity in all forms and encourage people to be themselves. My personal feeling is that the movement leads to more prejudice and stereotyping. Current texts on the topic mostly talk about *differences* between groups, when it seems to me that we should be talking what we have *in common*. The emphasis on differences leads to fear, not to acceptance of others. Different is not crazy or immoral; it's just different. We need to learn to let people be different without fearing them.

A second lesson is that *we can learn something from almost anyone*. Have you ever gotten into a conversation with a Jehovah's Witness? Most evangelicals consider them deluded heretics and shut the door in their faces, but—whether we agree with their doctrine or not—we could learn a lot from their commitment, perseverance in hardship, and training techniques. One thing is certain: we will never impress a Jehovah's Witness with our faith by shutting the door in his or her face.

A third lesson is that *people have no obligation to listen to us until we listen to them*. I had a student about three semesters ago, whom I'll call "Corey," who wrote some hard-core cynical stuff in a journal assignment. It really bothered me, so I wrote him an email to discuss it. In the email, I gave him an offer: I told him we could talk about anything he desired—no subjects were off limits—as long as we could have a true dialogue. In other words, we would listen to each other first. It was hard for me not to just quote the Bible as we talked, but thankfully I recognized that it was not the time for that approach. By the end of the semester, Corey had taken some big steps on a journey of faith. It required listening to him first, and I am so thankful that I did not just say what had first come to mind.

Finally, I have learned that *if you treat people with respect, they'll respect you.* I believe that this is the missing element in the current emphasis on diversity. Treat people like human beings regardless of color or creed, and they will do the same for you. That sounds a lot like the Golden Rule, does it not? Try it!

Well, here we are, at the end of this part of the journey. I didn't set out to write an exhaustive text, but something short, powerful, and practical that you could put into practice. Thank you for reading my book. My prayer is that God will use it to help you develop your own theology of counseling.

Reflection: What is your immediate reaction when confronted with people who are different from you? What type of difference bothers you the most?

References

Gallup (2006). "Religion Most Important to Blacks, Women, and Older Americans." Frank Newport, November 29, 2006. http://www.gallup.com/poll/25585/Religion-Most-Important-Blacks-Women-Older-Americans.aspx.

Horton-Parker, Radha J. & R. Charles Fawcett (2010). *Spirituality in Counseling and Psychotherapy: The Face-Spirit Model*. Denver: Love Press.

Jones, Stanton L. & Richard E. Butman (1991). *Modern Psychotherapies: A Comprehensive Christian Appraisal*. Downers Grove, IL: Intervarsity Press.

Kelly, Eugene W., Jr. (1995). *Spirituality and Religion in Counseling and Psychotherapy: Diversity in Theory and Practice*. Alexandria, VA: American Counseling Association.

McMinn, Mark R. (1986). *Psychology, Theology, and Spirituality in Christian Counseling.* Carol Stream, IL: Tyndale House Publishers. Pargament, Kenneth I. (1997). *The Psychology of Religion and Coping: Theory, Research, Practice.* New York: Guilford Press.

Thompson, Oscar W. & Carolyn T. Ritzman (1981). *Concentric Circles of Concern: Seven Stages for Making Disciples.* Nashville, TN: Broadman & Holman Press.

Appendix

Reading List for EDU 685

Religion, Spirituality, and Diversity in the Helping Professions

Alter, M.G. (1994). *Resurrection Psychology*. Chicago: Loyola University Press.

Arterburn, S. & Felton, J. (2001). *Toxic Faith: Experiencing Healing from Painful Spiritual Abuse*. Colorado Springs, CO: Waterbrook Press.

Arterburn, S. & Felton, J. (2001). *More Jesus, Less Religion: Moving from Rules to Relationship*. Colorado Springs, CO: Waterbrook Press.

Arterburn, S (2005). *Healing Is a Choice*. Nashville, TN: Thomas Nelson.

Benson, H. (1996). *Timeless Healing*. New York: Scribner Press.

Carlson, R. (1997). *Don't Sweat the Small Stuff*. New York: Hyperion.

Carlson, R. & Carlson, K. (2008). *An Hour to Live, an Hour to Love*. New York: Hyperion.

Chamberlin, P. (2005). *Talking About Good and Bad Without Getting Ugly*. Downers Grove, IL: Intervarsity Press.

Cloud, H. & Townsend, J. (1995). *Twelve "Christian" Beliefs that Can Drive You Crazy*. Grand Rapids, MI: Zondervan.

Colby, K.W. (2001). *Teachers & Religion in Public Schools*. Pasadena, CA: Light in Learning Press.

Corey, G., Corey, M.S. & Callanan, P. (1998). *Issues and Ethics in the Helping Professions*. Pacific Grove, CA: Brooks/Cole.

Covey, S.R. (1989). *The 7 Habits of Highly Effective People*. New York: Simon & Schuster.

Dossey, L. (1991). *Prayer Is Good Medicine*. San Francisco: Harper Collins.

Lass, M. (2004). *Understanding the Koran: A Quick Christian Guide to the Muslim Holy Book*. Grand Rapids, MI: Zondervan.

Emmons, R.A. (1999). *The Psychology of Ultimate Concerns*. New York: Guilford.

Frame, M.W. (2003). *Integrating Religion and Spirituality into Counseling*. Pacific Grove, CA: Brooks/Cole.

Finley, J. (2004). *Christian Meditation*. San Francisco: HarperCollins.

Griffith J.L. & Griffith, M. E. (2001). *Encountering the Sacred in Psychotherapy*. New York: Guilford.

Helmeke, K.B. & Ford, C.F. (2006). *The Therapist's Notebook for Integrating Spirituality and Counseling*. New York: Haworth Press.

Johnson E.I. & Jones, S.L. (2000). *Psychology & Christianity: Four Views*. Downers Grove, IL: Intervarsity Press.

Johnson, R. (1999). *Your Personality and the Spiritual Life*. Gainesville, FL: Center for the Application of Psychological Type (CAPT).

Jones, P. (2006). *Is Belief in God Good, Bad, or Irrelevant?* Downers Grove, IL: Intervarsity Press.

Jones, S.L. & Yarhouse, M.A. (2000). *Homosexuality: The Use of Research in the Church's Moral Debate*. Downers Grove, IL: Intervarsity Press.

Kise, J.A.G., Stark, D. & Hirsh, S.K. (1996). *LifeKeys: Discover Who You Are*. Minneapolis, MN: Bethany House.

Keith, K.M. (2001). *Anyway: the Paradoxical Commandments*. New York: Putnam.

Kelly, E.W. (1995). *Spirituality and Religion in Counseling and Psychotherapy*. Alexandria, VA: American Counseling Association.

Koenig, H.G. (1997). *Is Religion Good for Your Health? The Effects of Religion on Physical and Mental Health*. New York: The Haworth Pastoral Press.

Koenig, H.G. (1999). *The Healing Power of Faith*. New York: Simon & Schuster.

Larimore, W. (2003). *Ten Essentials of Highly Healthy People*. Grand Rapids, MI: Zondervan.

CPSIA information can be obtained at www.ICGtesting.com
Printed in the USA
BVOW072336070513

320131BV00002B/10/P

9 781414 122632